THE U.S BAN ON KASPERSKY SOFTWARE

Unraveling The High-Stakes Battle Over Cybersecurity, National Security & International Relations In the Digital Age

Laura D. Everett

All rights reserved. No part of this publication may be reproduced, distributed, or transmitted in any form or by any means, including photocopying, recording, or other electronic or mechanical methods, without the prior written permission of the copyright owner, except in the case of brief quotations embodied in critical reviews and certain other noncommercial uses permitted by copyright law.

Copyright © 2024 by Laura D. Everett

Table of Content

Introduction   7
    The Unfolding Cybersecurity Landscape   7
    Overview of Kaspersky and Its Global Presence   10
    The U.S. Government's Stand on Cybersecurity Threats   14

Chapter 1: The Origins of Kaspersky   19
    Founding and Early Years   19
    Growth and Expansion into Global Markets   22
    Innovations and Key Products   26

Chapter 2: Kaspersky's Contributions to Cybersecurity   31
    Major Threats Identified and Neutralized   31
    Collaborations with Global Security Agencies   35
    Public Perception and Industry Accolades   40

Chapter 3: The U.S. Ban: A Detailed Account   45
    Timeline Leading to the Ban   45
    Key Statements from U.S. Officials   48
    Immediate Reactions from Kaspersky   52

Chapter 4: Analyzing the Security Risk Claims   58
    Evidence and Allegations Against Kaspersky   58
    The Role of Geopolitics in Cybersecurity   61
    Expert Opinions and Analysis   65

Chapter 5: Impact on American Consumers and Businesses   69
    What the Ban Means for Current Users   69

Alternatives to Kaspersky Software 72
Steps for Transitioning to New Security Solutions 76
Chapter 6: The Global Repercussions **81**
International Reactions and Responses 81
The Broader Implications for Russian Tech Companies 84
Cybersecurity Policies in the Wake of the Ban 88
Chapter 7: Kaspersky's Response and Legal Battle 93
Statements and Actions by Kaspersky 93
Legal Options and Potential Outcomes 96
The Future of Kaspersky in the Global Market 100
Chapter 8: A Historical Perspective **104**
Previous Government Actions Against Kaspersky 104
The Evolution of Cyber Threats and Responses 107
Lessons from Past Cybersecurity Incidents 111
Conclusion: Looking Forward: The Future of Cybersecurity **117**
Emerging Threats and Challenges 117
Innovations in Cyber Defense 120
The Role of Government and Private Sector Collaboration 125

Introduction

The Unfolding Cybersecurity Landscape

The digital age, with its myriad advancements and conveniences, has ushered in an era where data is both a powerful asset and a potential liability. As businesses, governments, and individuals increasingly rely on digital infrastructure, the importance of cybersecurity has grown exponentially. This unfolding landscape is characterized by a relentless battle between those striving to protect information and those seeking to exploit vulnerabilities.

In recent years, high-profile cyber attacks have made headlines, highlighting the pervasive threat that cybercriminals pose. From ransomware attacks crippling city governments and hospitals to sophisticated espionage operations targeting sensitive state secrets, the spectrum of cyber threats is vast and ever-evolving. The complexity and scale of these attacks have revealed significant weaknesses in global cybersecurity defenses, prompting a reevaluation of how we safeguard our digital world.

The motivations behind cyberattacks are as varied as the attackers themselves. Some are driven by financial gain, leveraging ransomware to extort money from desperate victims. Others, particularly state-sponsored actors, are motivated by espionage, seeking to gain strategic advantages by infiltrating foreign networks. Ideological motivations also play a role, with hacktivists targeting entities they perceive as morally or politically objectionable.

The response to this growing threat has been multifaceted. Governments have established dedicated cybersecurity agencies and passed legislation aimed at bolstering defenses and punishing perpetrators. The private sector, particularly companies at the forefront of technology and finance, has invested heavily in cybersecurity measures. Yet, despite these efforts, the landscape remains fraught with challenges. The sophistication of cyber threats continues to outpace many defensive measures, and the interconnected nature of the global digital infrastructure means that a breach in one area can have far-reaching consequences.

Moreover, the COVID-19 pandemic has accelerated digital transformation across industries, further complicating the cybersecurity landscape. Remote work and increased reliance on cloud services have expanded the attack surface, providing cybercriminals with more opportunities to exploit vulnerabilities. This rapid shift has forced organizations to adapt quickly, often prioritizing functionality over security, which can lead to oversight and increased risk.

In this dynamic and high-stakes environment, the importance of robust cybersecurity cannot be overstated. As we move forward, the challenge will be to stay one step ahead of cyber adversaries, developing and implementing innovative solutions that protect our data and infrastructure. The unfolding cybersecurity landscape is a testament to the ongoing battle between innovation and exploitation, a battle that will shape the future of our digital world.

Overview of Kaspersky and Its Global Presence

Founded in 1997 by Eugene Kaspersky, Kaspersky Lab has grown from a small startup into a global powerhouse in the cybersecurity industry. With its headquarters in Moscow, Russia, the company has expanded its footprint to over 200 countries and territories, boasting more than 400 million individual users and over 240,000 corporate clients. Kaspersky's rise to prominence has been marked by its innovative approach to cybersecurity and its relentless pursuit of excellence in protecting against digital threats.

Kaspersky's product portfolio is extensive, encompassing antivirus solutions, internet security suites, and advanced threat detection systems. The company is renowned for its cutting-edge research and development, consistently staying ahead of emerging threats. Kaspersky's antivirus software, in particular, has garnered widespread acclaim for its effectiveness in detecting and neutralizing malware, earning numerous awards and certifications from independent testing organizations.

A cornerstone of Kaspersky's success has been its Global Research and Analysis Team (GReAT), a group of elite cybersecurity experts dedicated to uncovering and analyzing sophisticated cyber threats. GReAT has been instrumental in identifying and dissecting some of the most complex malware campaigns, including Stuxnet,

Duqu, Flame, and Gauss. Their work has not only enhanced Kaspersky's products but has also contributed to the broader understanding of cyber threats within the cybersecurity community.

Despite its achievements, Kaspersky's global presence has not been without controversy. The company's roots in Russia have led to scrutiny and suspicion, particularly from Western governments. Concerns about potential ties to the Russian government and the possibility of Kaspersky being compelled to assist in espionage activities have cast a shadow over its operations. These concerns culminated in the U.S. government's decision to ban the use of Kaspersky software by federal agencies in 2017, citing national security risks.

Kaspersky has vehemently denied any allegations of wrongdoing, maintaining that it operates independently and is committed to transparency. In an effort to allay fears and demonstrate its integrity, Kaspersky launched its Global Transparency

Initiative in 2017. This initiative includes measures such as relocating data processing to Switzerland, opening Transparency Centers for independent review, and engaging third-party auditors to assess the company's practices.

The impact of these efforts on Kaspersky's reputation has been mixed. While some stakeholders have been reassured by the company's transparency measures, others remain cautious, particularly in light of the geopolitical tensions between Russia and the West. Nevertheless, Kaspersky continues to play a vital role in the cybersecurity landscape, providing essential protection to millions of users worldwide.

As we explore deeper into the story of Kaspersky, it is important to understand both the technical prowess and the geopolitical complexities that define its journey. The company's evolution from a modest antivirus developer to a global cybersecurity leader is a testament to its resilience and innovation, even as it navigates the challenging waters of international politics and security concerns.

The U.S. Government's Stand on Cybersecurity Threats

In an era where cyber threats are pervasive and increasingly sophisticated, the U.S. government has taken a proactive stance in addressing cybersecurity risks. The federal government's approach to cybersecurity is multi-faceted, involving legislation, regulatory measures, and collaboration with both domestic and international partners. Central to this strategy is the protection of critical infrastructure, safeguarding sensitive information, and ensuring the resilience of the nation's digital assets.

One of the key agencies at the forefront of this effort is the Cybersecurity and Infrastructure Security Agency (CISA), established in 2018. CISA's mission is to lead the national effort to understand, manage, and reduce risk to the nation's cyber and physical infrastructure. This includes working closely with state and local governments, private sector entities, and international allies to enhance cybersecurity practices and respond to emerging threats.

The U.S. government's stance on cybersecurity has also been shaped by a series of high-profile cyber incidents. Attacks such as the SolarWinds breach, the Colonial Pipeline ransomware attack, and various state-sponsored espionage operations have underscored the need for robust defensive measures. In response, the government has implemented a range of initiatives designed to bolster cybersecurity across sectors. These include the Cybersecurity Executive Order, which mandates improvements in software supply chain security, incident reporting, and the adoption of zero-trust architecture.

Another significant aspect of the U.S. government's approach is its stance on foreign technology companies operating within its borders. The concerns about potential espionage and influence by foreign adversaries have led to scrutiny and regulatory action against companies perceived as security risks. The decision to ban Kaspersky software is a prominent example of this policy in action. The ban reflects the government's broader strategy to mitigate risks associated with foreign influence and ensure the integrity of the nation's digital infrastructure.

The rationale behind the Kaspersky ban is rooted in the belief that the company's Russian origins pose an inherent risk. U.S. officials have argued that Russian law could compel Kaspersky to cooperate with the Russian government, potentially leading to the exploitation of its software for espionage or other malicious activities. While specific evidence of wrongdoing by Kaspersky has not been publicly disclosed, the decision is based on a precautionary principle, aiming to eliminate potential vulnerabilities before they can be exploited.

This precautionary approach has sparked debate within the cybersecurity community. Critics argue that the ban may be more politically motivated than based on concrete evidence, and that it sets a precedent for similar actions against other foreign tech companies. Supporters, however, contend that the potential risks are too great to ignore and that the government's primary responsibility is to protect national security.

The U.S. government's stance on cybersecurity threats is not static; it evolves in response to the changing landscape of digital threats and technological advancements. As cyber adversaries continue to innovate, so too must the strategies and measures employed to defend against them. The ban on Kaspersky is one chapter in this ongoing narrative, highlighting the complexities and challenges inherent in safeguarding the digital realm.

In the chapters that follow, we will explore the specifics of the Kaspersky ban by exploring the evidence, implications, and responses from various stakeholders and understanding the broader context of the U.S. government's cybersecurity strategy.

Chapter 1: The Origins of Kaspersky

Founding and Early Years

The story of Kaspersky begins in the early 1990s, a time when the internet was still in its infancy, and the concept of cybersecurity was not yet a household term. It was during this period that Eugene Kaspersky, a young cryptographer with a passion for computer technology, stumbled upon a piece of malware that would change the course of his life. This discovery ignited a fascination with computer viruses and a determination to find ways to combat them.

Eugene Kaspersky was working at a Russian defense institute when he encountered the "Cascade" virus on his personal computer in 1989. Intrigued and alarmed by the virus's capabilities, Kaspersky began to study its structure and behavior. His efforts led to the creation of a rudimentary antivirus tool that successfully neutralized the threat. This initial success fueled Kaspersky's desire to explore deeper into the world of cybersecurity.

In 1991, Kaspersky joined KAMI Information Technologies Center, where he continued to develop antivirus software. His growing expertise in the field earned him a reputation as a leading authority on computer viruses. Recognizing the potential for a dedicated antivirus company, Kaspersky, along with a group of like-minded colleagues, founded Kaspersky Lab in 1997. The company's mission was clear: to protect computer users from the growing threat of malware.

The early years of Kaspersky Lab were marked by rapid innovation and a relentless pursuit of excellence. The team operated out of a modest office in Moscow, working tirelessly to refine their antivirus solutions. They faced numerous challenges, including limited resources and a highly competitive market. However, their dedication and technical prowess soon began to pay off.

One of Kaspersky Lab's first major breakthroughs came in 1998 with the release of their flagship product, Kaspersky Anti-Virus (KAV). This software quickly gained recognition for its effectiveness and reliability, earning accolades from independent testing organizations. Kaspersky Anti-Virus set a new standard in the industry, positioning the company as a formidable player in the global cybersecurity market.

The founders' commitment to innovation and quality was a driving force behind Kaspersky Lab's early success. Eugene Kaspersky's vision extended beyond merely creating effective antivirus software; he aimed to build a comprehensive cybersecurity ecosystem capable of addressing a wide range of digital threats. This holistic approach would become a hallmark of Kaspersky Lab's operations, guiding the company's growth and development in the years to come.

Growth and Expansion into Global Markets

As Kaspersky Lab solidified its reputation in the Russian market, the company began to set its sights on international expansion. The turn of the millennium marked a pivotal moment in Kaspersky's journey as it embarked on a strategic plan to extend its reach beyond Russia's borders. The company's goal was to become a global leader in cybersecurity, providing advanced protection to users worldwide.

The early 2000s saw Kaspersky Lab establish a network of regional offices and partnerships across Europe, Asia, and the Americas. This expansion was fueled by a combination of strategic marketing, localized product offerings, and a strong commitment to customer support. Kaspersky's ability to adapt to the unique needs of different markets played a crucial role in its successful globalization.

One of the key strategies employed by Kaspersky Lab was to participate actively in international cybersecurity conferences and trade shows. These events provided a platform for the company to showcase its cutting-edge technology and engage with potential clients and partners. By fostering relationships with industry leaders and government agencies, Kaspersky Lab was able to build a robust international presence.

The company's growth was not without its challenges. Navigating the regulatory landscapes of different countries required careful planning and compliance with various legal frameworks. Additionally, the competitive nature of the global cybersecurity market meant that Kaspersky Lab had to continually innovate to stay ahead of rivals. Despite these obstacles, the company's relentless pursuit of excellence ensured its steady ascent in the industry.

By the mid-2000s, Kaspersky Lab had firmly established itself as a global cybersecurity powerhouse. The company's products were widely recognized for their superior protection capabilities and user-friendly design. Kaspersky Lab's success was underscored by numerous awards and certifications from independent testing organizations, which attested to the efficacy and reliability of its solutions.

The global financial crisis of 2008 presented both challenges and opportunities for Kaspersky Lab. While economic downturns typically lead to reduced IT budgets, the growing awareness of cyber threats during this period heightened demand for robust cybersecurity solutions. Kaspersky Lab capitalized on this trend by offering cost-effective, high-quality products that appealed to budget-conscious organizations.

Kaspersky Lab's expansion into the enterprise market marked another significant milestone in its growth trajectory. The company's solutions for businesses and critical infrastructure sectors gained traction, further solidifying its reputation as a trusted provider of comprehensive cybersecurity services. This diversification of its product portfolio allowed Kaspersky Lab to cater to a broader range of clients, from individual consumers to large corporations.

The establishment of research and development centers in key regions around the world also played a pivotal role in Kaspersky Lab's expansion. These centers enabled the company to tap into local talent pools and leverage regional expertise to enhance its products and services. The global R&D network became a cornerstone of Kaspersky Lab's innovation strategy, ensuring that the company remained at the forefront of the cybersecurity industry.

Innovations and Key Products

Innovation has always been at the heart of Kaspersky Lab's success. The company's relentless pursuit of cutting-edge technology and its commitment to staying ahead of emerging threats have resulted in a series of groundbreaking products and solutions. From advanced antivirus software to comprehensive security suites, Kaspersky Lab's innovations have set new benchmarks in the cybersecurity industry.

One of the most significant innovations in Kaspersky Lab's history was the development of its heuristic analysis technology. Unlike traditional antivirus software that relied solely on known virus signatures, heuristic analysis allowed Kaspersky's solutions to detect and neutralize previously unknown threats. This proactive approach significantly enhanced the effectiveness of Kaspersky's products, providing users with a higher level of protection.

Kaspersky Lab's introduction of cloud-based threat intelligence marked another major advancement. The company's cloud infrastructure, known as Kaspersky Security Network (KSN), collects and analyzes vast amounts of data from millions of sensors worldwide. This real-time threat intelligence enables Kaspersky's solutions to detect and respond to emerging threats faster than ever before. The integration of cloud-based analytics has become a cornerstone of modern cybersecurity practices, and Kaspersky Lab was at the forefront of this shift.

In addition to its core antivirus offerings, Kaspersky Lab has developed a range of specialized security solutions tailored to different user needs. For instance, Kaspersky Internet Security provides comprehensive protection for online activities, including banking and shopping, while Kaspersky Total Security offers additional features such as password management and file encryption. These products are designed to provide a holistic security experience, addressing a wide spectrum of digital risks.

Kaspersky Lab's commitment to innovation extends beyond software development. The company has invested heavily in cybersecurity research, leading to the discovery and analysis of some of the most sophisticated malware campaigns in history. The work of Kaspersky's Global Research and Analysis Team (GReAT) has been instrumental in uncovering threats such as Stuxnet, Flame, and Gauss. These discoveries have not only advanced the field of cybersecurity but have also underscored Kaspersky Lab's position as a leader in threat intelligence.

Another key innovation from Kaspersky Lab is its Endpoint Detection and Response (EDR) solutions. EDR technology provides organizations with advanced tools to detect, investigate, and respond to complex threats targeting their endpoints. Kaspersky's EDR solutions leverage machine learning and behavioral analysis to identify suspicious activity, enabling security teams to swiftly mitigate potential breaches. This capability is crucial in an era where targeted attacks and advanced persistent threats (APTs) are becoming increasingly prevalent.

Kaspersky Lab has also made significant strides in securing the rapidly expanding Internet of Things (IoT) ecosystem. Recognizing the unique challenges posed by connected devices, the company has developed specialized solutions to protect IoT environments from cyber threats. Kaspersky's IoT security offerings include firmware analysis, network segmentation, and anomaly detection, providing comprehensive protection for smart homes, industrial systems, and critical infrastructure.

The company's commitment to user education and awareness is another aspect of its innovative approach. Kaspersky Lab offers a range of resources, including webinars, whitepapers, and training programs, to help users understand and mitigate cyber risks. By empowering users with knowledge and best practices, Kaspersky Lab aims to create a more secure digital landscape for everyone.

As Kaspersky Lab continues to innovate, its focus remains on addressing the evolving threat landscape with solutions that are both effective and user-friendly. The company's dedication to research, development, and education ensures that it remains at the cutting edge of cybersecurity. By staying true to its founding principles of excellence and innovation, Kaspersky Lab continues to protect millions of users worldwide from the ever-present dangers of the digital age.

Chapter 2: Kaspersky's Contributions to Cybersecurity

Major Threats Identified and Neutralized

Kaspersky Lab has made significant contributions to cybersecurity through its identification and neutralization of some of the most sophisticated and damaging cyber threats in history. The company's Global Research and Analysis Team (GReAT), composed of elite cybersecurity experts, has been at the forefront of these efforts, uncovering and analyzing complex malware that has targeted governments, businesses, and individuals around the world.

One of the earliest and most notable threats that Kaspersky identified was the Stuxnet worm in 2010. Stuxnet was a game-changer in the world of cybersecurity, as it was the first known malware to specifically target industrial control systems. Its discovery highlighted the potential for cyber weapons to cause physical damage to critical infrastructure. Kaspersky's analysis of Stuxnet provided invaluable insights into its sophisticated design and operation, demonstrating the company's capability to tackle unprecedented threats.

Following Stuxnet, Kaspersky played a crucial role in uncovering other major cyber threats such as Duqu and Flame. Duqu, discovered in 2011, was closely related to Stuxnet and was used for espionage purposes, collecting information from industrial control systems to facilitate future attacks. Flame, identified in 2012, was an exceptionally complex espionage toolkit capable of recording audio, capturing screenshots, and stealing data. Kaspersky's detailed analyses of these threats shed light on their intricate functionalities and the potential actors behind them.

In 2012, Kaspersky's discovery of the Gauss malware further underscored its expertise in dealing with advanced cyber espionage tools. Gauss targeted the banking sector in the Middle East, aiming to steal sensitive financial information and credentials. The malware's sophistication and stealthy nature highlighted the growing trend of state-sponsored cyber espionage. Kaspersky's ability to dissect and understand Gauss provided critical intelligence to the global cybersecurity community.

Kaspersky's proactive approach to threat hunting also led to the identification of the Equation Group, one of the most sophisticated and elusive cyber threat actors ever discovered. Revealed in 2015, the Equation Group was linked to a series of highly advanced cyber espionage campaigns dating back to at least 2001. Their tools and techniques were so sophisticated that they were considered nearly impossible to detect. Kaspersky's uncovering of the Equation Group's activities highlighted the extent to which nation-states invest in cyber capabilities.

Another significant contribution came in 2017 with the identification of the WannaCry ransomware. This global ransomware attack affected hundreds of thousands of computers across more than 150 countries, crippling businesses, healthcare systems, and government services. Kaspersky's rapid response and analysis were instrumental in understanding the ransomware's propagation mechanisms and advising affected organizations on mitigation strategies.

Kaspersky's work in identifying and neutralizing these major threats has not only protected countless systems from compromise but has also advanced the collective understanding of cyber threats. The company's detailed reports and threat intelligence have become essential resources for cybersecurity professionals worldwide, fostering a collaborative approach to defending against malicious actors.

Through its relentless pursuit of cybersecurity excellence, Kaspersky has demonstrated a profound commitment to making the digital world safer. The company's ability to identify and neutralize major threats has solidified its reputation as a leader in the field, providing a crucial line of defense in the ever-evolving battle against cybercrime.

Collaborations with Global Security Agencies

Kaspersky Lab's contributions to cybersecurity extend beyond its technical prowess; the company has also played a significant role in fostering collaboration with global security agencies. These partnerships have been instrumental in enhancing the collective ability to respond to cyber threats, sharing critical intelligence, and developing coordinated defense strategies.

One of the key aspects of Kaspersky's collaborative efforts is its participation in global cybersecurity forums and initiatives. The company regularly engages with international organizations such as INTERPOL, Europol, and the United Nations to share insights and threat intelligence. These collaborations have enabled a more comprehensive understanding of cyber threats and facilitated joint operations to combat cybercrime.

For instance, Kaspersky has worked closely with INTERPOL on various projects aimed at enhancing global cybersecurity capabilities. In 2014, Kaspersky signed an agreement with INTERPOL to provide cyber threat intelligence and support the organization's cybercrime investigations. This partnership has led to the successful disruption of numerous cybercriminal operations, demonstrating the effectiveness of international cooperation.

Kaspersky's collaboration with Europol has also yielded significant results. The company has been involved in Europol's Joint Cybercrime Action Taskforce (J-CAT), which focuses on combating transnational cybercrime. By sharing threat intelligence and expertise, Kaspersky has helped Europol identify and dismantle cybercriminal networks, leading to the arrest of key figures involved in various illicit activities.

In addition to law enforcement agencies, Kaspersky collaborates with national cybersecurity centers and regulatory bodies. The company has established partnerships with entities such as the UK's National Cyber Security Centre (NCSC) and Germany's Federal Office for Information Security (BSI). These collaborations involve sharing threat intelligence, conducting joint research, and developing best practices to enhance national cybersecurity resilience.

Kaspersky's commitment to transparency has also played a crucial role in building trust and fostering collaboration. In 2017, the company launched its Global Transparency Initiative, aimed at providing greater visibility into its operations and processes. As part of this initiative, Kaspersky opened Transparency Centers in Switzerland, Spain, and Malaysia, where government stakeholders and partners can review the company's source code, software updates, and threat detection rules. This openness has helped address concerns about potential security risks and reinforced Kaspersky's dedication to accountability.

Furthermore, Kaspersky has engaged in numerous public-private partnerships to strengthen cybersecurity across various sectors. The company collaborates with industry groups, academic institutions, and non-profit organizations to advance research and education in cybersecurity. These partnerships have resulted in the development of innovative solutions and the dissemination of best practices, contributing to a more secure digital environment.

One notable example of Kaspersky's public-private collaboration is its involvement in the No More Ransom initiative, launched in 2016 in partnership with Europol, the Dutch National Police, and other cybersecurity companies. This initiative provides free decryption tools and resources to help victims of ransomware recover their data without paying ransoms. Kaspersky's technical expertise and commitment to fighting cybercrime have been instrumental in the success of this initiative, which has helped countless individuals and organizations.

Kaspersky's collaborative approach extends to its efforts in addressing emerging threats. The company actively participates in international working groups and task forces focused on issues such as IoT security, AI in cybersecurity, and the protection of critical infrastructure. By sharing knowledge and fostering dialogue, Kaspersky contributes to the development of global standards and policies that enhance cybersecurity resilience.

Kaspersky Lab's collaborations with global security agencies have significantly advanced the fight against cyber threats. Through partnerships with law enforcement, national cybersecurity centers, and industry groups, the company has facilitated the sharing of critical intelligence, supported joint operations, and contributed to the development of best practices. These collaborative efforts underscore Kaspersky's commitment to making the digital world safer and more secure for everyone.

Public Perception and Industry Accolades

Kaspersky Lab's journey through the cybersecurity landscape has been marked by significant achievements, yet it has also faced challenges in terms of public perception. The company's reputation is a complex interplay of its undeniable contributions to cybersecurity and the geopolitical tensions that have influenced its standing in the global market.

From its inception, Kaspersky Lab has been highly regarded for its technical excellence and innovative solutions. The company's antivirus software has consistently received top ratings from independent testing organizations such as AV-TEST, AV-Comparatives, and Virus Bulletin. These accolades reflect Kaspersky's commitment to providing high-quality protection against a wide range of cyber threats. The company's products are known for their robust detection capabilities, user-friendly interfaces, and minimal impact on system performance.

Kaspersky's contributions to the field of cybersecurity research have also earned it significant respect within the industry. The company's Global Research and Analysis Team (GReAT) has uncovered some of the most sophisticated cyber threats, providing valuable insights that have advanced the understanding of malware and cyber espionage. Reports and analyses published by Kaspersky are frequently cited in academic papers, industry studies, and by other cybersecurity professionals, underscoring the company's role as a thought leader in the field.

Despite these accomplishments, Kaspersky Lab has faced scrutiny due to its Russian origins. Concerns about potential ties to the Russian government and the possibility of the company being compelled to assist in espionage activities have led to a complex public perception, particularly in Western countries. These concerns came to a head in 2017 when the U.S. government banned the use of Kaspersky software by federal agencies, citing national security risks.

The U.S. ban significantly impacted Kaspersky's public perception and market presence. While the company has vehemently denied any wrongdoing and has taken steps to increase transparency, including moving some of its data processing to Switzerland and opening Transparency Centers, the geopolitical climate has continued to pose challenges. The ban also sparked similar actions in other countries, further complicating Kaspersky's efforts to maintain a positive global image.

In response to these challenges, Kaspersky has focused on reinforcing its commitment to transparency and trust. The Global Transparency Initiative, launched in 2017, aims to address concerns by allowing independent reviews of the company's source code and operations. This initiative has been well-received by some stakeholders and has helped to mitigate some of the negative perceptions. However, the shadow of geopolitical tension remains a significant factor influencing public opinion.

Despite the hurdles, Kaspersky Lab's industry accolades continue to highlight its contributions and the quality of its products. The company has received numerous awards for innovation and excellence, including the SC Awards, InfoSec Awards, and Cybersecurity Excellence Awards. These honors reflect the industry's recognition of Kaspersky's ongoing efforts to advance cybersecurity and protect users from digital threats.

Moreover, Kaspersky's involvement in initiatives like No More Ransom and its extensive educational outreach programs have bolstered its reputation as a responsible and proactive player in the cybersecurity space. By providing free resources to ransomware victims and engaging in public awareness campaigns.

Chapter 3: The U.S. Ban: A Detailed Account

Timeline Leading to the Ban

The timeline leading to the U.S. ban on Kaspersky Lab software is a narrative marked by escalating tensions and mounting concerns over cybersecurity and national security. The story begins in the early 2010s, a period when cyber threats were becoming increasingly sophisticated and geopolitical dynamics were influencing the digital realm.

In 2015, the U.S. intelligence community began to express unease about the potential risks posed by Kaspersky Lab due to its headquarters in Moscow and perceived ties to the Russian government. These concerns were amplified by reports that Kaspersky's software, widely used across various sectors, could potentially be leveraged for espionage. The growing apprehension was set against the backdrop of a rapidly deteriorating relationship between the U.S. and Russia, particularly following Russia's annexation of Crimea in 2014 and its alleged interference in the 2016 U.S. presidential election.

The situation escalated in September 2017, when the Department of Homeland Security (DHS) issued a Binding Operational Directive (BOD) instructing all federal executive branch departments and agencies to identify and remove Kaspersky Lab products from their information systems. This directive was a response to perceived risks that Kaspersky's antivirus software could provide a conduit for Russian intelligence operations. DHS cited concerns that Russian laws could compel Kaspersky to assist the government in intercepting communications transiting Russian networks.

The directive required federal agencies to complete three actions: identify the use of Kaspersky products within 30 days, develop plans to remove and discontinue use of the products within 60 days, and begin the removal process within 90 days. This aggressive timeline underscored the urgency and seriousness with which the U.S. government viewed the threat.

Further stoking the fire, in October 2017, The Wall Street Journal reported that Russian hackers, allegedly using Kaspersky software, had stolen classified data from a National Security Agency (NSA) contractor's home computer. This incident added significant weight to the argument that Kaspersky posed a national security risk, although Kaspersky Lab denied any involvement and emphasized that any misuse of its software would have been without its knowledge or consent.

Throughout 2018, the controversy continued to unfold. In March, the U.S. government banned Kaspersky products from use in federal networks through the National Defense Authorization Act.

This legislative action solidified the earlier DHS directive and expanded the scope of the ban. Despite Kaspersky Lab's efforts to contest the decision, including a lawsuit against the U.S. government claiming the ban was unconstitutional, the U.S. District Court upheld the ban in May 2018, citing national security concerns.

The timeline leading up to the ban highlights a period of intense scrutiny and action, characterized by rapid policy developments and significant media coverage. Each step in this progression contributed to an environment where the perceived risks associated with Kaspersky Lab became a matter of urgent national security, culminating in the formal ban that reverberated through the cybersecurity industry.

Key Statements from U.S. Officials

The decision to ban Kaspersky Lab software was accompanied by numerous statements from U.S.

officials that underscored the gravity of the situation and the rationale behind the ban. These statements reflect a deep-seated concern about cybersecurity and national security, and they played a crucial role in shaping public and governmental opinion.

In September 2017, when the Department of Homeland Security issued its Binding Operational Directive, Acting Secretary Elaine Duke emphasized the imperative to protect federal information systems. She went on: "The department is concerned about the ties between certain Kaspersky officials and Russian intelligence and other government agencies, and requirements under Russian law that allow Russian intelligence agencies to compel assistance from Kaspersky and to intercept communications transiting Russian networks." This statement set the tone for the government's stance, highlighting both the specific concerns about Kaspersky's connections and the broader legal environment in Russia.

As the debate over Kaspersky intensified, other officials added their voices. In October 2017, Rob Joyce, the White House cybersecurity coordinator at the time, expressed the administration's concerns during a forum, stating, "It's more prudent to act now and mitigate the potential risk than to hope for the best. Kaspersky as a company has an excellent reputation in the industry, but when you look at the broad context of Russia's cyber activities, we need to be very cautious about allowing their software to interact with our most sensitive information."

In December 2017, during a Senate hearing on cybersecurity threats, Jeanette Manfra, Assistant Secretary for Cybersecurity and Communications at DHS, reiterated the potential risks posed by Kaspersky software. She said, "Given the grave concerns about the threat to our federal information systems, the department had to act decisively. We couldn't wait for a crisis to unfold; the potential for misuse of Kaspersky products to harm national security was too significant to ignore."

The legislative push to formalize the ban also saw strong statements from lawmakers. Senator Jeanne Shaheen, a leading advocate for the ban, stated in December 2017, "The case against Kaspersky is overwhelming. There's a clear and present danger to the United States from Kaspersky products, and the risk is unacceptable. We must ensure that our cybersecurity defenses are as robust and uncompromised as possible."

The U.S. government's position was further reinforced by intelligence community assessments. In a February 2018 hearing before the Senate Intelligence Committee, Director of National Intelligence Dan Coats discussed the broader context of Russian cyber activities, noting, "Russia is a full-scope cyber actor that poses a major threat to military, diplomatic, commercial, critical infrastructure sectors and U.S. government. The

50

use of Kaspersky software, given its headquarters and potential obligations to the Russian state, represents a significant risk that we cannot afford."

These statements collectively painted a picture of a government deeply concerned about the intersection of cybersecurity and national security. They highlighted the perceived inevitability of Russian influence over Kaspersky Lab and the potential for the software to be used as a tool of espionage. The narrative constructed by these statements not only justified the ban but also aimed to reassure the public and stakeholders that the actions taken were necessary to protect national interests.

Immediate Reactions from Kaspersky

The immediate reactions from Kaspersky Lab to the U.S. ban were marked by a mix of denial, defiance, and efforts to mitigate the damage to its reputation and business. The company's leadership, led by founder and CEO Eugene Kaspersky, took a proactive stance in addressing the allegations and defending the integrity of their operations.

In response to the DHS directive in September 2017, Kaspersky Lab issued a statement expressing disappointment and disagreement with the decision. The company emphasized its long-standing commitment to transparency and cooperation with international law enforcement agencies, including those in the U.S. The statement said, "Kaspersky Lab has never assisted, nor will it assist, any government in the globe with its cyber-espionage activities," the statement read. Eugene Kaspersky himself took to social media and the press to assert that his company was being unfairly targeted and that the allegations were unfounded.

In an open letter published on the company's website, Eugene Kaspersky addressed customers and partners directly, reassuring them of the company's dedication to safeguarding their data. He stated, "We at Kaspersky Lab have always been committed to defending our clients against cyberthreats, no matter where they come from or what they're used for. We have nothing to hide, and we are ready to show our source code and internal processes to prove that our actions are entirely above board."

As the controversy continued, Kaspersky Lab announced several measures aimed at restoring trust and transparency. In October 2017, the company unveiled its Global Transparency Initiative, which included the opening of Transparency Centers where government stakeholders and partners could review the company's source code, software updates, and threat detection rules. These centers were established in locations such as Zurich, Madrid, and Kuala Lumpur, with the goal of demonstrating the company's commitment to transparency and countering the allegations against it.

Eugene Kaspersky also embarked on a media campaign, giving interviews to major news outlets to clarify the company's position and counteract the negative publicity. He argued that the ban was politically motivated and not based on any concrete evidence of wrongdoing by Kaspersky Lab. In a notable interview with The Associated Press, he stated, "We are being accused without any evidence, and this is not fair. Our products are trusted by millions of users around the world, and we will continue to fight for the truth."

In addition to its public relations efforts, Kaspersky Lab took legal action to challenge the U.S. government's decision. In December 2017, the company filed a lawsuit against the Department of Homeland Security, seeking to overturn the ban. The lawsuit argued that the ban was unconstitutional and lacked substantive evidence to support the claims of a national security threat. Although the lawsuit was ultimately unsuccessful, it underscored Kaspersky's determination to defend its reputation and business interests.

Kaspersky Lab's immediate reactions also included efforts to reassure its existing customer base. The company provided detailed guidance on how users could continue to protect their systems, even in the face of the ban. For instance, they emphasized the importance of keeping their software updated and offered alternatives for users who might be concerned about the implications of the ban.

Despite the significant challenges posed by the U.S. ban, Kaspersky Lab's response highlighted the company's resilience and commitment to its principles. The combination of transparency initiatives, legal challenges, and proactive communication aimed to counteract the negative impact and preserve the trust of its global user base. While the U.S. ban undoubtedly affected

Kaspersky's market position, particularly in the United States, the company's immediate reactions demonstrated its resolve to continue operating as a leading cybersecurity provider.

Chapter 4: Analyzing the Security Risk Claims

Evidence and Allegations Against Kaspersky

The security risk claims against Kaspersky Lab are rooted in a complex web of allegations and circumstantial evidence, primarily centered on the company's ties to Russia and its potential susceptibility to influence by Russian intelligence agencies. The most prominent accusation is that Kaspersky's software could be used as a tool for espionage, given the company's origins and operational base in Moscow.

The U.S. Department of Homeland Security (DHS) and other federal entities pointed to the possibility that Kaspersky Lab might be compelled under Russian law to assist the government in intelligence-gathering activities. Russian federal law requires companies to assist the Federal Security Service (FSB) in state security matters, which fuels concerns that Kaspersky, whether willingly or under coercion, could be forced to facilitate espionage activities.

In 2017, allegations intensified when The Wall Street Journal reported that Russian hackers had used Kaspersky software to steal classified data from a National Security Agency (NSA) contractor's home computer. The report suggested that the hackers exploited the software to identify and exfiltrate sensitive information, raising alarms about the potential for Kaspersky products to serve as conduits for cyber espionage. This incident, although denied by Kaspersky, was cited as a critical factor in the U.S. government's decision to ban its software.

Adding to the allegations were reports that some senior Kaspersky employees had past associations with Russian military or intelligence services. This background fueled suspicions that the company could have covert links with the Russian state, further amplifying fears about its integrity and independence.

Despite these allegations, concrete evidence proving intentional misconduct or direct collusion with Russian intelligence by Kaspersky has not been publicly disclosed. Kaspersky Lab has repeatedly denied any wrongdoing, asserting that it has never assisted any government in cyber espionage and highlighting its commitment to transparency. The company points to its Global Transparency Initiative, which includes independent audits and reviews of its source code, as proof of its dedication to mitigating security concerns and building trust.

The lack of disclosed evidence has led to a polarized perception of Kaspersky. Critics argue that the potential risk is too significant to ignore, even without public proof, while supporters claim that the accusations are politically motivated and lack substantiation. The resulting dichotomy underscores the complexity and emotional charge surrounding the security risk claims against Kaspersky Lab, as stakeholders grapple with balancing cybersecurity, trust, and geopolitical influences.

The Role of Geopolitics in Cybersecurity

Geopolitics plays an increasingly crucial role in cybersecurity, influencing how nations perceive and respond to threats from foreign entities. The case of Kaspersky Lab is a vivid example of how geopolitical tensions can shape cybersecurity policies and practices, often leading to contentious and impactful decisions.

The U.S. ban on Kaspersky software is deeply rooted in the broader context of strained U.S.-Russia relations. Following Russia's annexation of Crimea in 2014 and the allegations of Russian interference in the 2016 U.S. presidential election, the U.S. government became increasingly wary of Russian influence and the potential for cyber operations to compromise national security. These geopolitical tensions created an environment of heightened suspicion and urgency to safeguard critical infrastructure from perceived threats.

The decision to ban Kaspersky software can be seen as part of a larger strategy to limit Russian technological influence and mitigate the risk of espionage. By restricting the use of Kaspersky products, the U.S. aimed to reduce the attack surface that could potentially be exploited by Russian state actors. This approach aligns with broader efforts to protect national security interests and maintain sovereignty in the digital domain.

However, the interplay between geopolitics and cybersecurity is not confined to the actions of any single nation. Countries worldwide are increasingly adopting protectionist measures, influenced by geopolitical considerations, to secure their digital ecosystems. This trend has led to the rise of national cybersecurity policies that prioritize domestic solutions over foreign technologies, sometimes at the expense of international cooperation and innovation.

Geopolitical dynamics also influence how cyber incidents are interpreted and addressed. Attribution of cyber attacks is inherently complex and often politically charged, with nations leveraging cyber incidents to advance their geopolitical agendas. The attribution of the 2016 election interference to Russian actors, for example, has had far reaching implications, leading to sanctions, diplomatic tensions, and a re-evaluation of cybersecurity alliances.

In the case of Kaspersky, geopolitics has not only driven the U.S. government's actions but also shaped public perception. The narrative surrounding Kaspersky is colored by the broader geopolitical context, with many viewing the company through the lens of U.S.-Russia relations. This geopolitical framing complicates the objective assessment of security risks and highlights the challenge of disentangling technical considerations from political influences.

The role of geopolitics in cybersecurity underscores the need for a nuanced and balanced approach. While national security concerns are paramount, there is also a risk that overzealous protectionist measures could stifle innovation and collaboration. As cybersecurity threats continue to evolve, finding a harmonious balance between safeguarding national interests and fostering international cooperation will be crucial to building a resilient and secure digital future.

Expert Opinions and Analysis

The debate surrounding Kaspersky Lab and its alleged security risks has elicited a wide range of expert opinions and analyses, reflecting the complexity and multifaceted nature of the issue. Cybersecurity professionals, industry analysts, and policy experts have weighed in, offering diverse perspectives that highlight both the technical and geopolitical dimensions of the controversy.

Many cybersecurity experts acknowledge Kaspersky Lab's technical prowess and contributions to the field. The company is widely respected for its research capabilities and its role in uncovering significant cyber threats such as Stuxnet, Duqu, and Flame. These experts argue that Kaspersky's products are among the best in the industry in terms of malware detection and threat mitigation. They emphasize that the company's technical expertise should not be overshadowed by geopolitical concerns, and that its Global

Transparency Initiative is a positive step towards building trust.

However, other experts underscore the inherent risks associated with using software from a company based in a nation with adversarial relations to the U.S. They argue that the potential for state interference cannot be ignored, especially given the legal environment in Russia, which could compel companies to cooperate with government intelligence operations. These experts suggest that, even in the absence of direct evidence, the precautionary principle should apply, and the potential risks warrant the actions taken by the U.S. government.

Policy analysts and geopolitical experts also provide important context to the discussion. They point out that the ban on Kaspersky is part of a broader trend of increasing digital protectionism and strategic decoupling in the tech sector. The U.S. decision is seen as a move to bolster national cybersecurity by reducing reliance on foreign technologies that could be exploited for espionage. These analysts argue that in the current geopolitical climate, trust in digital infrastructure is paramount, and measures like the Kaspersky ban are necessary to maintain national security.

Critics of the ban, including some legal experts, argue that the actions against Kaspersky set a concerning precedent. They highlight the lack of transparent evidence presented to justify the ban and warn that such measures could be perceived as politically motivated, potentially leading to retaliatory actions by other countries. This perspective suggests that the U.S. government's approach could undermine global cybersecurity cooperation and foster an environment of mutual suspicion.

From a business perspective, industry analysts note that the ban has significant implications for Kaspersky's market position, particularly in the

U.S. and other Western markets. The company's efforts to counteract the negative impact, such as relocating data processing and opening Transparency Centers, are seen as strategic moves to regain trust and sustain its global operations. These analysts highlight the resilience of Kaspersky's business model and its continued innovation despite the geopolitical challenges.

The expert opinions and analyses surrounding Kaspersky Lab highlight the intersection of technical excellence and geopolitical realities. While the company's contributions to cybersecurity are widely recognized, the potential risks associated with its Russian origins cannot be dismissed in the current geopolitical context. The diverse perspectives underscore the need for a balanced approach that considers both security imperatives and the importance of maintaining global cooperation in the fight against cyber threats.

Chapter 5: Impact on American Consumers and Businesses

What the Ban Means for Current Users

The U.S. government's ban on Kaspersky software has significant implications for American consumers and businesses that rely on the company's antivirus and cybersecurity solutions. Effective from July 20, the ban prohibits the sale of Kaspersky products in the United States and extends to both individual users and corporate entities. For those currently using Kaspersky software, this decision marks a turning point that demands immediate attention and action.

For individual consumers, the most pressing concern is the security of their personal data. While the ban does not criminalize the continued use of Kaspersky products, it does mean that after September 29, Kaspersky will no longer be permitted to provide software updates and security patches to U.S. customers. This cessation of updates is critical because it leaves systems vulnerable to new threats and exploits that emerge daily. Without timely updates, antivirus software becomes significantly less effective, potentially exposing users to cyber-attacks, malware, and data breaches.

Businesses face an even more complex scenario. Many enterprises depend on Kaspersky's advanced security solutions to protect sensitive information and maintain the integrity of their operations. The ban affects a broad spectrum of businesses, from small enterprises to large corporations, and even critical infrastructure organizations. For these entities, the inability to receive updates and support from Kaspersky presents a substantial risk. Cybersecurity is a foundational element of business continuity, and any disruption can lead to significant financial losses, reputational damage, and regulatory repercussions.

Moreover, the transition away from Kaspersky software entails logistical and operational challenges. Businesses must allocate resources to identify, procure, and implement alternative security solutions, all while ensuring that their networks remain protected throughout the process. This transition can be resource-intensive, requiring technical expertise and potentially involving downtime that can disrupt normal business activities.

Emotionally, the ban has stirred anxiety and uncertainty among users who have trusted Kaspersky for years. The company's reputation for robust cybersecurity solutions means that many users now face the daunting task of finding an equivalent alternative. This transition period can be stressful, as users must navigate the crowded cybersecurity market to identify products that offer the same level of protection and reliability.

In summary, the U.S. ban on Kaspersky software places American consumers and businesses at a crossroads. The immediate need to switch to alternative security solutions to avoid vulnerabilities is paramount. The decision underscores the critical nature of staying informed about geopolitical factors that can impact technology choices and emphasizes the importance of proactive cybersecurity measures in safeguarding personal and corporate data.

Alternatives to Kaspersky Software

As American consumers and businesses move away from Kaspersky software due to the U.S. government's ban, the need for robust and reliable alternative cybersecurity solutions becomes imperative. Fortunately, the cybersecurity market offers a wide array of options, each with its strengths and features designed to protect against evolving threats.

One of the leading alternatives is **NortonLifeLock** (formerly known as Symantec). Norton's suite of security products is well-regarded for its comprehensive protection, including antivirus, anti-malware, firewall, and identity theft protection. Norton offers both individual and business solutions, ensuring that all users can find a product tailored to their specific needs. Its reputation for excellent customer support and frequent updates makes it a strong contender for those seeking to replace Kaspersky.

Another prominent option is **McAfee**. Known for its powerful antivirus and internet security solutions, McAfee provides extensive coverage that includes real-time threat detection, ransomware protection, and secure cloud storage. McAfee's solutions are particularly popular among businesses due to their scalability and robust management features, making them suitable for both small businesses and large enterprises.

For users looking for a high level of customization and control over their security settings, **Bitdefender** is a compelling choice. Bitdefender offers a range of products that cater to various user requirements, from basic antivirus protection to advanced cybersecurity suites with features such as VPN, parental controls, and anti-tracker capabilities. Bitdefender's strong performance in independent tests for malware detection and minimal impact on system performance makes it an attractive alternative.

Trend Micro is another noteworthy alternative, particularly known for its strong anti-phishing capabilities and comprehensive protection against ransomware and other sophisticated threats. Trend Micro's security solutions are user-friendly and offer real-time protection, making them suitable for both individuals and businesses.

ESET is also a respected name in the cybersecurity industry, offering a range of products that combine powerful malware protection with a light system footprint. ESET's NOD32 technology is highly praised for its detection accuracy and minimal impact on system resources, making it a good choice for users who need robust protection without compromising system performance.

For those seeking open-source solutions, **ClamAV** is a viable option. While it may not offer the same level of polish and user-friendliness as commercial products, ClamAV provides effective antivirus protection and is particularly popular in server environments and among tech-savvy users who prefer customizable solutions.

The cybersecurity market provides a wealth of alternatives to Kaspersky, each with unique features and strengths. Whether users prioritize comprehensive protection, user-friendliness, customization, or cost-effectiveness, there are suitable options available to meet their needs. The key is to carefully evaluate each product's capabilities and align them with individual or organizational requirements to ensure continued protection in an increasingly digital world.

Steps for Transitioning to New Security Solutions

Transitioning from Kaspersky software to a new security solution is a critical process that requires careful planning and execution to ensure continued protection without compromising system integrity. For both individuals and businesses, following a structured approach can mitigate risks and facilitate a smooth transition.

The first step is to **assess current security needs**. Users should evaluate their existing cybersecurity requirements, considering factors such as the number of devices, types of data being protected, and specific security features needed (e.g., anti-phishing, firewall, VPN). This assessment helps in selecting an alternative solution that aligns with their needs and provides equivalent or superior protection compared to Kaspersky.

Next, it is essential to **research and select a new cybersecurity solution**. As outlined in the previous section, there are numerous alternatives available, each with its strengths. Users should compare features, pricing, user reviews, and independent test results to make an informed decision. Trial versions of software can be beneficial in assessing usability and compatibility with existing systems.

Once a new solution is chosen, users should **prepare for the transition.** This involves backing up important data to prevent loss during the transition process. For businesses, this step may also include notifying employees and stakeholders about the impending change and providing guidance on the transition process.

The actual transition begins with the **uninstallation of Kaspersky software**. It is crucial to fully remove Kaspersky from all devices to avoid potential conflicts with the new security software. Kaspersky provides tools and instructions for thorough uninstallation, which should be followed meticulously.

After uninstalling Kaspersky, users should **install and configure the new security solution**. This step involves downloading the new software from a trusted source, following installation instructions, and configuring settings according to security needs. For businesses, this may include setting up centralized management consoles and deploying the software across multiple devices.

Post-installation, it is vital to **run initial scans and updates**. Users should perform comprehensive system scans to ensure there are no lingering threats that might have gone undetected. Updating the new software to the latest version ensures that all recent patches and threat definitions are in place, providing maximum protection.

During the initial period of using the new software, users should **monitor system performance and security alerts**. This helps in identifying any issues early and making necessary adjustments. For businesses, continuous monitoring is crucial to ensure that the new solution integrates well with other IT systems and does not interfere with business operations.

Finally, it is important to **stay informed and proactive**. Cybersecurity is an ongoing process, and staying updated on the latest threats and best practices is essential. Regularly updating software, performing routine scans, and being vigilant about security alerts can help maintain a robust defense against cyber threats.

In summary, transitioning from Kaspersky to a new security solution involves assessing needs, selecting the right alternative, carefully uninstalling the old software, installing and configuring the new solution, and maintaining vigilant monitoring. By following these steps, individuals and businesses can ensure continued protection and minimize disruption during the transition.

Chapter 6: The Global Repercussions

International Reactions and Responses

The U.S. government's ban on Kaspersky software reverberated around the globe, eliciting a spectrum of reactions from various countries, organizations, and industry stakeholders. This landmark decision underscored the intertwining of cybersecurity and geopolitics, prompting international discourse on the balance between national security and technological reliance.

Many allied nations expressed understanding and support for the U.S. decision, recognizing the potential risks posed by foreign-based cybersecurity firms with perceived ties to adversarial governments. Countries within the European

Union, in particular, scrutinized their own use of Kaspersky products. Germany and the UK, for example, undertook reviews of Kaspersky software in their critical infrastructure sectors. Although not all nations implemented outright bans, there was a noticeable shift towards caution and increased regulatory oversight.

Conversely, some countries viewed the U.S. ban with skepticism, perceiving it as a politically motivated maneuver rather than a purely security-driven decision. Russia, predictably, condemned the ban, arguing that it was part of a broader strategy to undermine Russian businesses on the international stage. The Russian government emphasized Kaspersky's contributions to global cybersecurity and called for evidence to substantiate the claims of espionage risks.

In Asia, reactions were mixed. Countries like Japan and South Korea, which have strong security alliances with the U.S., considered the implications for their cybersecurity policies and procurement strategies. Meanwhile, China, already embroiled in its own technological standoff with the U.S., observed the situation with a strategic lens, analyzing how similar actions might be directed against its tech giants.

The cybersecurity industry itself was divided. Some companies saw the ban as an opportunity to capture market share previously held by Kaspersky, while others were concerned about the precedent it set for the politicization of cybersecurity. The potential for reciprocal actions by other nations loomed large, threatening to fragment the global cybersecurity landscape.

Consumer reactions were also varied. Some users, particularly those in the U.S., heeded the government's warnings and transitioned to alternative security solutions. Others, loyal to Kaspersky due to its proven track record and technical excellence, viewed the ban as an overreach, continuing to use the software despite the official stance.

Overall, the international responses to the U.S. ban on Kaspersky software highlight the complex interplay between national security, trust in technology, and global geopolitical dynamics. The decision not only influenced cybersecurity practices but also sparked broader conversations about the future of international cooperation and competition in the digital age.

The Broader Implications for Russian Tech Companies

The U.S. ban on Kaspersky software casts a long shadow over the broader landscape of Russian tech companies, signaling potential challenges and reshaping their strategies in the global market. This action underscored the vulnerabilities of tech firms operating in politically charged environments and prompted a reevaluation of how these companies navigate international relations and regulatory landscapes.

For Russian tech companies, the ban serves as a stark reminder of the geopolitical risks that can abruptly disrupt business operations. It highlights the precarious balance they must maintain between adhering to domestic regulations and gaining the trust of international customers. In response, many Russian tech firms have sought to enhance transparency and implement measures aimed at reassuring global clients. These efforts include conducting third-party audits, establishing data centers outside Russia, and participating in international cybersecurity collaborations.

However, the broader implications extend beyond immediate business adjustments. The ban has prompted a reconsideration of the global tech supply chain and the dependencies that various nations have on foreign technologies. This introspection is particularly pertinent for countries that rely heavily on Russian software and IT services. As a result, there is a growing trend towards diversification, with nations seeking to reduce their reliance on any single foreign technology provider to mitigate the risk of future disruptions.

The ripple effect of the ban has also influenced the strategic direction of Russian tech companies. To counteract the negative impact, these firms are increasingly pivoting towards markets less influenced by U.S. policies, such as parts of Asia, Africa, and Latin America. In these regions, Russian tech companies are emphasizing their technological prowess and cost-competitiveness to establish a foothold and expand their customer base.

Moreover, the ban has accelerated the push for technological self-sufficiency within Russia. The Russian government has intensified efforts to develop domestic alternatives to foreign technologies, fostering innovation and investment in the local tech ecosystem. This move is part of a broader strategy to ensure that critical infrastructure and national security are not compromised by reliance on potentially hostile foreign tech providers.

For international tech companies, the U.S. ban on Kaspersky serves as a cautionary tale about the importance of geopolitical risk management. It underscores the need for companies to be aware of and responsive to the geopolitical environments in which they operate. This awareness includes understanding the potential implications of their business practices and affiliations, as well as the importance of maintaining a reputation for independence and trustworthiness.

The U.S. ban on Kaspersky software has far-reaching implications for Russian tech companies, influencing their global strategies, market focus, and operational practices. It highlights the intricate link between technology and geopolitics and the necessity for tech firms to navigate this landscape with agility and foresight.

Cybersecurity Policies in the Wake of the Ban

The U.S. ban on Kaspersky software has catalyzed a significant shift in cybersecurity policies worldwide, prompting governments and organizations to reassess their strategies and frameworks for ensuring digital security. The decision has underscored the importance of evaluating not just the technical capabilities of cybersecurity solutions but also the geopolitical contexts in which these solutions are developed and maintained.

One of the most immediate policy responses has been the tightening of procurement rules and regulations regarding foreign technology products. Governments are increasingly prioritizing national security considerations in their cybersecurity policies, requiring more stringent vetting processes for software and hardware used in critical infrastructure. This includes conducting comprehensive risk assessments that take into account the country of origin of the technology providers and their potential susceptibility to foreign government influence.

The ban has also accelerated the trend towards digital sovereignty, with many nations seeking to reduce their dependency on foreign cybersecurity solutions. This shift is driven by the desire to mitigate risks associated with geopolitical tensions and to ensure that critical digital infrastructure remains secure and resilient. Countries are investing in the development of domestic cybersecurity industries, encouraging local innovation and supporting homegrown tech companies to build robust, independent digital ecosystems.

In addition to national policies, the ban has influenced international cybersecurity collaborations. Countries are recognizing the need for enhanced cooperation and information sharing to address the complex and borderless nature of cyber threats. Multilateral initiatives and agreements are being strengthened to facilitate joint efforts in threat intelligence, incident response, and cybersecurity capacity building. These collaborations aim to foster a more unified and effective approach to global cybersecurity challenges.

At the organizational level, businesses are revisiting their cybersecurity policies and practices to ensure compliance with evolving regulations and to maintain robust defenses against potential threats. This includes adopting more comprehensive security frameworks, conducting regular audits and assessments, and implementing best practices for data protection and incident response. The emphasis is on building resilience and adaptability to rapidly changing threat landscapes.

Moreover, the ban has highlighted the importance of transparency and accountability in the cybersecurity industry. Tech companies are increasingly expected to demonstrate their commitment to security and privacy through independent audits, certifications, and adherence to international standards. This transparency is crucial for building and maintaining trust with customers, partners, and regulators.

Educational and training initiatives are also gaining prominence as part of the broader cybersecurity policy landscape. Governments and organizations are investing in programs to enhance cybersecurity awareness and skills among the workforce. These initiatives aim to create a culture of security, equipping individuals with the knowledge and tools to identify and mitigate cyber risks effectively.

In summary, the U.S. ban on Kaspersky software has had profound implications for cybersecurity policies around the world. It has driven a reevaluation of procurement practices, spurred investments in digital sovereignty, strengthened international collaborations, and emphasized the importance of transparency and education. These policy shifts reflect a growing recognition of the need for a holistic and proactive approach to cybersecurity in an increasingly interconnected and geopolitically complex world.

Chapter 7: Kaspersky's Response and Legal Battle

Statements and Actions by Kaspersky

In the wake of the U.S. government's ban on its software, Kaspersky responded with a mix of defiance, clarification, and a call for fairness. The company's leadership, led by founder Eugene Kaspersky, swiftly issued statements to address the accusations and reassure their global customer base. They emphasized Kaspersky's longstanding commitment to transparency and cybersecurity excellence, highlighting their substantial contributions to identifying and mitigating global cyber threats.

Eugene Kaspersky himself took to social media and press interviews to assert that the ban was politically motivated and lacked substantial evidence. He underscored that Kaspersky has never engaged in any actions that would compromise the security of its users and reiterated the company's willingness to cooperate with any investigations to prove its innocence. The firm emphasized that it operates with the highest ethical standards, with its data processing and storage facilities strategically located outside Russia to address concerns about data sovereignty and privacy.

Kaspersky also pointed to its Global Transparency Initiative, launched in 2017, as a testament to its dedication to openness and security. This initiative involved relocating core infrastructure to Switzerland, opening Transparency Centers where partners and government stakeholders can review the company's source code, and subjecting its operations to independent audits. These measures, according to Kaspersky, were designed to dispel doubts about its integrity and demonstrate its commitment to protecting users regardless of geopolitical tensions.

Furthermore, Kaspersky launched a public relations campaign aimed at both consumers and businesses, reassuring them of the continued safety and reliability of its products. The company offered resources to assist users in understanding the situation, including detailed FAQs, webinars, and direct support channels. These efforts were geared towards maintaining customer trust and minimizing the potential fallout from the ban.

In addition to public statements, Kaspersky took immediate steps to mitigate the impact on its business operations. They began exploring new markets less influenced by U.S. policies and intensified efforts to strengthen relationships with existing customers in Europe, Asia, and Latin America. The company also worked on diversifying its product portfolio, investing in next-generation cybersecurity technologies to stay competitive in the evolving digital landscape.

Kaspersky's response to the U.S. ban has been multifaceted, combining public reassurance, transparency efforts, and strategic business adjustments. The company has consistently positioned itself as a victim of geopolitical maneuvering, seeking to uphold its reputation and sustain its global presence amidst the controversy.

Legal Options and Potential Outcomes

Facing a ban from one of its largest markets, Kaspersky explored various legal avenues to challenge the U.S. government's decision. The company's legal team began by scrutinizing the rationale behind the ban, aiming to identify potential grounds for appeal. Kaspersky's primary argument centered on the lack of concrete evidence presented by the U.S. authorities to substantiate the claims of national security risks.

One of the first steps Kaspersky took was to file formal objections with relevant U.S. regulatory bodies, requesting a review of the decision. The company argued that the ban was not only unfair but also detrimental to the principles of free trade and competition. Kaspersky emphasized its rigorous compliance with international cybersecurity standards and its proactive measures to ensure transparency and security.

In parallel, Kaspersky considered legal action in the form of lawsuits challenging the ban's legality. Potential claims included violations of due process and lack of substantive evidence to support the accusations. The company aimed to demonstrate that the decision was arbitrary and lacked a factual basis, seeking to overturn the ban or at least mitigate its impact through legal means.

The outcomes of these legal efforts could vary widely. If successful, Kaspersky could secure a reversal or modification of the ban, allowing it to continue operations in the U.S. market under certain conditions. This outcome would hinge on the ability to convince courts or regulatory bodies that the ban was unwarranted and harmful to both the company and its customers.

Alternatively, even if the legal challenges do not result in a complete overturn of the ban, they might still achieve a compromise. For example, Kaspersky could negotiate conditions under which it could operate, such as enhanced oversight or additional transparency measures. This middle ground could help restore some level of market access while addressing security concerns.

However, there is also the possibility that legal challenges could be unsuccessful, cementing the ban and forcing Kaspersky to fully exit the U.S. market. Such an outcome would necessitate a significant strategic shift, focusing on other regions and potentially rebranding to overcome the stigma associated with the ban.

Regardless of the specific legal outcomes, Kaspersky's pursuit of these options reflects its determination to fight for its reputation and market position. The company's proactive legal strategy underscores its commitment to countering what it perceives as an unjust and politically motivated action.

Kaspersky's legal battle against the U.S. ban involves a multifaceted approach aimed at challenging the decision's validity and seeking remedies through both regulatory appeals and litigation. The potential outcomes range from full reinstatement in the U.S. market to strategic compromises or a complete exit, each carrying significant implications for the company's future.

The Future of Kaspersky in the Global Market

The future of Kaspersky in the global market is shaped by a combination of resilience, adaptation, and strategic innovation. Despite the significant setback posed by the U.S. ban, the company remains a formidable player in the cybersecurity industry, leveraging its technical expertise and extensive global presence to navigate this challenging landscape.

One of the key strategies for Kaspersky is diversification. The company is expanding its product offerings beyond traditional antivirus software to include advanced cybersecurity solutions such as threat intelligence services, endpoint detection and response (EDR), and security orchestration, automation, and response (SOAR) platforms. These innovations cater to the growing demand for comprehensive cybersecurity frameworks capable of addressing complex and evolving threats.

Geographically, Kaspersky is intensifying its focus on regions less affected by U.S. policies. Europe, Asia, and Latin America represent significant growth opportunities, where Kaspersky continues to maintain a strong reputation for quality and reliability. The company is investing in localized support and marketing efforts to strengthen its foothold in these markets, ensuring that regional concerns and regulatory requirements are addressed.

Moreover, Kaspersky is enhancing its collaborations with global security agencies and industry partners. By participating in international cybersecurity initiatives and forums, the company aims to reinforce its commitment to global security and demonstrate its collaborative spirit. These partnerships are crucial for maintaining credibility and fostering trust with stakeholders worldwide.

Another critical aspect of Kaspersky's future strategy is emphasizing transparency and independence. The Global Transparency Initiative remains a cornerstone of this approach, with the company continuing to open Transparency Centers in strategic locations and inviting independent audits of its processes and source code. These measures are designed to reassure customers and regulators that Kaspersky operates with integrity and is not influenced by any government, including Russia's.

Innovation also plays a central role in Kaspersky's vision for the future. The company is investing heavily in research and development to stay ahead of emerging cyber threats. This includes exploring new technologies such as artificial intelligence and machine learning to enhance threat detection and response capabilities. By pushing the boundaries of cybersecurity innovation, Kaspersky aims to maintain its competitive edge and appeal to a broad spectrum of customers, from individual users to large enterprises.

Despite the challenges, Kaspersky's commitment to quality and innovation provides a solid foundation for its continued success. The company's ability to adapt to geopolitical pressures, diversify its offerings, and maintain a strong presence in key markets underscores its resilience. As the cybersecurity landscape evolves, Kaspersky's proactive strategies and unwavering focus on excellence will be crucial in navigating the complexities of the global market.

Chapter 8: A Historical Perspective

Previous Government Actions Against Kaspersky

Kaspersky, a global cybersecurity giant, has faced scrutiny from governments long before the recent U.S. ban. The company's journey has been marked by a series of confrontations with state authorities, driven by geopolitical tensions and concerns over digital sovereignty.

One of the earliest and most significant actions came in September 2017, when the Trump administration banned U.S. federal agencies from using Kaspersky software. This move was prompted by fears that Kaspersky could be coerced into assisting Russian intelligence operations. The ban was a clear signal of the growing mistrust between the U.S. and Russian technological entities. U.S. officials cited concerns that Kaspersky's antivirus software, widely used and deeply integrated into many systems, could potentially be leveraged for espionage.

Kaspersky responded by vehemently denying any ties to Russian intelligence and by filing lawsuits against the U.S. government, challenging the ban's legality and demanding evidence to support the accusations. Although the company's legal efforts did not overturn the ban, they highlighted the complex interplay between cybersecurity, national security, and international politics.

In Europe, reactions to Kaspersky have been more mixed but similarly cautious. For instance, in 2018, the Dutch government announced plans to phase out the use of Kaspersky software in critical infrastructure. The move was precautionary, driven by the same concerns that had motivated the U.S. ban. However, other European countries have taken a more measured approach, opting for rigorous scrutiny and risk assessments rather than outright bans.

These government actions against Kaspersky reflect broader trends in the cybersecurity landscape, where the origins and affiliations of technology companies are increasingly scrutinized. The fear is not just about potential backdoors or direct espionage but also about the ability of foreign states to exert influence over companies that operate within their jurisdiction.

For Kaspersky, these challenges have prompted a series of strategic responses. The company has implemented measures to increase transparency, such as moving some data processing operations to Switzerland and opening transparency centers where stakeholders can review its code and operations. These actions aim to rebuild trust and demonstrate that Kaspersky operates independently of any government influence.

The historical perspective on government actions against Kaspersky reveals a pattern of escalating scrutiny and protective measures. These actions are part of a broader narrative of digital sovereignty and cybersecurity in an era where technological dependencies intersect with national security concerns. Understanding this context is crucial for appreciating the complexities faced by companies like Kaspersky as they navigate the global cybersecurity landscape.

The Evolution of Cyber Threats and Responses

The world of cyber threats has evolved dramatically over the past few decades, transforming from relatively simple malware and viruses to sophisticated, state-sponsored cyber warfare. This evolution has necessitated equally sophisticated responses, reshaping the cybersecurity landscape and the roles of companies like Kaspersky.

In the early days of the internet, cyber threats were primarily the domain of individual hackers and small groups seeking notoriety or financial gain. The infamous Morris Worm of 1988, one of the first widely recognized malware outbreaks, caused significant disruption but was more a demonstration of vulnerability than a targeted attack. Responses during this era were relatively straightforward: developing antivirus software and educating users about basic cyber hygiene.

As the internet grew, so did the complexity and frequency of cyber threats. The turn of the millennium saw the rise of more organized cybercrime, with groups using increasingly sophisticated methods to steal data and money. The Love Bug virus in 2000, which caused an estimated $10 billion in damages globally, exemplified the escalating scale of cyber threats. Companies like Kaspersky emerged as key players in the fight against these evolving dangers, developing advanced antivirus solutions and beginning to incorporate heuristic analysis to detect previously unknown threats.

The 2000s also marked the beginning of a new era: cyber warfare and espionage. State-sponsored attacks became more prevalent, targeting critical infrastructure, governmental institutions, and major corporations. The Stuxnet worm in 2010, widely believed to be a joint U.S.-Israeli operation targeting Iran's nuclear program, underscored the devastating potential of cyber weapons. This era demanded a more comprehensive approach to cybersecurity, involving not just technological defenses but also international cooperation and policy development.

In response to these advanced threats, cybersecurity companies had to innovate rapidly. Kaspersky, for instance, developed extensive threat intelligence networks and began offering sophisticated security solutions beyond traditional antivirus software. These solutions included endpoint detection and response (EDR) systems, threat intelligence services, and advanced malware analysis tools.

The evolution of cyber threats has also led to the rise of public-private partnerships in cybersecurity. Governments and private companies now collaborate more closely to share information about emerging threats and develop coordinated responses. The establishment of national cybersecurity centers and international frameworks for cyber defense reflects this integrated approach.

Today, the cybersecurity landscape is characterized by a perpetual arms race between attackers and defenders. Cyber threats continue to grow in complexity, with trends such as ransomware-as-a-service, supply chain attacks, and AI-driven malware. In response, cybersecurity firms like Kaspersky are investing heavily in research and development to stay ahead of these threats, incorporating artificial intelligence and machine learning into their detection and response systems.

The evolution of cyber threats and responses highlights the dynamic nature of cybersecurity. It is a field that demands constant vigilance, innovation, and collaboration. As threats continue to evolve, so too must the strategies and technologies deployed to combat them, ensuring that the digital world remains as secure as possible.

Lessons from Past Cybersecurity Incidents

Past cybersecurity incidents offer valuable lessons for both individuals and organizations, shaping our understanding of vulnerabilities, threats, and effective defense strategies. By analyzing these incidents, we can identify patterns and principles that are crucial for developing robust cybersecurity practices.

One of the earliest and most influential cybersecurity incidents was the Morris Worm of 1988. Released by a graduate student, the worm inadvertently caused significant disruption by exploiting vulnerabilities in UNIX systems. The incident underscored the importance of patch management and the need for systems to have fail-safes that prevent a single vulnerability from being widely exploited. It also highlighted the necessity of having effective incident response plans in place.

The Love Bug virus of 2000 further emphasized the human factor in cybersecurity. Spread through email attachments with enticing subject lines, it relied on social engineering to propagate. This incident demonstrated that technical defenses alone are insufficient; user education and awareness are critical components of cybersecurity. Organizations learned the importance of training employees to recognize phishing attempts and other forms of social engineering.

The Stuxnet worm, discovered in 2010, provided a stark lesson in the potential for cyber weapons to target critical infrastructure. Allegedly developed by the U.S. and Israel to sabotage Iran's nuclear program, Stuxnet was a sophisticated attack that exploited zero-day vulnerabilities and used digital certificates to appear legitimate. This incident highlighted the need for robust security measures in industrial control systems and the importance of securing the supply chain to prevent the introduction of malicious software.

Another pivotal incident was the 2017 WannaCry ransomware attack, which affected hundreds of thousands of computers in over 150 countries. WannaCry exploited a vulnerability in Windows operating systems, which had been publicly disclosed by the hacking group Shadow Brokers. The global impact of WannaCry underscored the critical importance of timely patching and updating of systems. It also brought to light the necessity of having comprehensive backup solutions to mitigate the effects of ransomware.

The 2020 SolarWinds attack, one of the most sophisticated and far-reaching cyber espionage campaigns, taught vital lessons about supply chain security and the potential for widespread impact from a single compromised vendor. Attackers inserted malicious code into SolarWinds' Orion software, which was then distributed to numerous high-profile clients, including government agencies and large corporations. This incident emphasized the need for stringent security measures across the entire supply chain and the importance of monitoring and auditing third-party software.

These past incidents collectively highlight several key lessons for cybersecurity:

1. **Patch Management:** Keeping systems and software up to date is fundamental to protecting against known vulnerabilities.

2. **User Education:** Training users to recognize and respond appropriately to social engineering tactics is crucial.

3. **Incident Response:** Having a well-defined incident response plan can significantly mitigate the impact of an attack.

4. **Supply Chain Security:** Ensuring the security of third-party vendors and their products is vital to overall cybersecurity.

5. **Comprehensive Backup Solutions:** Regularly backing up data can prevent ransomware attacks from causing catastrophic data loss.

In conclusion, the lessons learned from past cybersecurity incidents are invaluable for shaping current and future defense strategies. By understanding the vulnerabilities exploited in these attacks and the responses that proved effective, organizations can build more resilient systems and better prepare for the ever-evolving landscape of cyber threats.

Conclusion: Looking Forward: The Future of Cybersecurity

Emerging Threats and Challenges

As we look toward the future of cybersecurity, emerging threats and challenges present a complex and ever-evolving landscape. The digital world is becoming increasingly interconnected, and with this interconnectedness comes a broader array of vulnerabilities and potential attack vectors.

One of the most pressing emerging threats is the rise of artificial intelligence (AI) and machine learning (ML) in cyberattacks. While these technologies offer significant benefits for cybersecurity defense, they can also be weaponized by attackers. AI-driven malware can adapt and evolve, making it harder to neutralize and detect.

This sophistication means that traditional signature-based detection methods will likely become less effective, necessitating more advanced behavioral analysis techniques.

Another significant challenge is the increasing prevalence of ransomware-as-a-service (RaaS). This model allows even those with minimal technical skills to launch sophisticated ransomware attacks, democratizing cybercrime and increasing the volume of attacks. Ransomware attacks are becoming more targeted, focusing on critical infrastructure, healthcare systems, and large corporations where the impact and the potential ransom can be much greater.

The expansion of the Internet of Things (IoT) also presents a formidable challenge. With billions of devices connected to the internet, each representing a potential entry point for attackers, securing the IoT ecosystem is a monumental task. Many IoT devices lack robust security measures, making them attractive targets for cybercriminals. The potential for massive, distributed denial-of-service (DDoS) attacks using IoT botnets is a particular concern.

Furthermore, the geopolitical landscape continues to influence cyber threats. State-sponsored attacks are likely to increase, with nations using cyber capabilities as tools of espionage, sabotage, and influence. Critical infrastructure, such as power grids, water supplies, and communication networks, remains a high-risk target due to the potential for causing widespread disruption and chaos.

Social engineering attacks are also evolving, becoming more sophisticated and harder to detect. Phishing campaigns now often use deepfake technology to create convincing but fake audio and video, tricking even the most cautious individuals. The lines between truth and deception are increasingly blurred, making it more challenging to discern legitimate communications from fraudulent ones.

In response to these emerging threats, the cybersecurity industry must continuously innovate and adapt. Proactive threat hunting, advanced threat intelligence, and the development of new defensive technologies are critical. Collaboration across industries and borders is essential to share knowledge, tools, and strategies to combat these global threats. As the landscape of cyber threats continues to evolve, so too must our approaches to defending against them, ensuring that we stay one step ahead of the adversaries.

Innovations in Cyber Defense

The future of cybersecurity lies in innovation, driven by the relentless need to stay ahead of increasingly sophisticated cyber threats. As attackers evolve their tactics, so too must the tools and strategies designed to thwart them. Several key innovations are shaping the next generation of cyber defense, promising more robust and proactive protection mechanisms.

Machine Learning (ML) and Artificial Intelligence (AI) are at the forefront of these innovations. AI and ML can analyze vast amounts of data far quicker and more accurately than humans, identifying patterns and anomalies that may indicate a cyber threat. By leveraging these technologies, cybersecurity systems can detect and respond to threats in real-time, often before human analysts are even aware of them. This capability is particularly crucial for identifying zero-day vulnerabilities and sophisticated, previously unknown attack vectors.

Behavioral analytics is another promising innovation. Traditional cybersecurity defenses often rely on predefined signatures to detect malware, which can be ineffective against new or modified threats. Behavioral analytics, however, focuses on identifying unusual activity patterns that deviate from normal behavior. This approach allows for the detection of advanced persistent threats (APTs) and insider threats that might bypass traditional security measures. By understanding what constitutes normal behavior for users and systems, deviations can be flagged and investigated promptly.

Quantum computing, while still in its early stages, represents a potential revolution in cybersecurity. Current encryption techniques may be broken by quantum computers, hence creating quantum-resistant encryption algorithms is necessary. On the flip side, quantum technology also promises more robust encryption techniques that could secure data against future cyber threats. Researchers and cybersecurity professionals are already working on developing and testing these quantum-resistant algorithms to prepare for the advent of quantum computing.

Blockchain technology offers another innovative approach to cybersecurity. Known primarily for its application in cryptocurrencies, blockchain's decentralized and immutable ledger can enhance security in various contexts. For example, blockchain can ensure the integrity and transparency of transactions and communications, making it much harder for cybercriminals to alter or forge data. This technology is particularly useful in securing supply chains, digital identity verification, and ensuring the authenticity of software updates.

Furthermore, advancements in automation and orchestration are enhancing incident response capabilities. Automated systems can quickly isolate infected systems, mitigate threats, and initiate recovery processes without the need for human intervention. This speed and efficiency are critical in minimizing the impact of cyberattacks and reducing downtime.

Lastly, the development of cybersecurity mesh architectures (CSMA) is gaining traction. This approach involves creating a flexible, scalable, and reliable cybersecurity control mesh that integrates security tools and policies across various environments. It allows for centralized management and decentralized enforcement, providing comprehensive security coverage for complex, distributed IT environments.

The future of cyber defense is being shaped by a wave of technological innovations. AI and ML, behavioral analytics, quantum computing, blockchain technology, automation, and cybersecurity mesh architectures are all contributing to more advanced, proactive, and resilient cybersecurity strategies. These innovations are essential to counter the evolving threat landscape and ensure the protection of critical digital assets in an increasingly connected world.

The Role of Government and Private Sector Collaboration

Effective cybersecurity in the modern world requires robust collaboration between governments and the private sector. This partnership is essential for developing comprehensive strategies to protect against the increasingly sophisticated and pervasive nature of cyber threats. The symbiotic relationship between public and private entities leverages the strengths of both, creating a unified front against cyber adversaries.

Governments play a crucial role in setting regulatory frameworks and standards that ensure a baseline level of cybersecurity across industries. By establishing policies and guidelines, governments can drive the adoption of best practices and enforce compliance with security protocols. Regulatory measures such as the General Data Protection Regulation (GDPR) in Europe and the Cybersecurity Information Sharing Act (CISA) in the United States exemplify efforts to enhance cybersecurity resilience through legislation. These regulations mandate stringent security measures and promote transparency, ensuring that organizations prioritize the protection of sensitive data.

On the other hand, the private sector is often at the forefront of technological innovation, developing cutting-edge solutions to address emerging cyber threats. Companies like Kaspersky, among others, invest heavily in research and development to stay ahead of cyber adversaries. Their expertise and technological advancements are invaluable in creating effective cybersecurity defenses. By collaborating with government agencies, these companies can share critical threat intelligence, enabling a more proactive and informed approach to cybersecurity.

One of the key aspects of government and private sector collaboration is information sharing. Cyber threats are global and constantly evolving, making timely and accurate information crucial for effective defense. Governments and private companies must work together to share threat intelligence, incident reports, and best practices. Information sharing initiatives, such as the Cyber Threat Alliance (CTA) and the National Cyber Security Centre's (NCSC) information sharing partnerships, facilitate this exchange of knowledge, helping to create a collective defense against cyber threats.

Joint training exercises and simulations are another vital component of this collaboration. By conducting cybersecurity drills and simulations, both government and private sector entities can test their response capabilities, identify weaknesses, and improve coordination during actual incidents. These exercises help build trust and understanding between different organizations, ensuring a more cohesive and effective response during a cyber crisis.

Furthermore, public-private partnerships can drive innovation in cybersecurity. Governments can provide funding and support for research initiatives, fostering the development of new technologies and solutions. Collaborative projects, such as the U.S. Department of Defense's Defense Advanced Research Projects Agency (DARPA) programs, bring together government agencies, private companies, and academic institutions to tackle complex cybersecurity challenges.

In the realm of critical infrastructure protection, collaboration is particularly crucial. Critical sectors such as energy, healthcare, finance, and transportation are prime targets for cyberattacks. The private companies operating in these sectors often possess specialized knowledge and resources necessary for robust cybersecurity. Government agencies can support these efforts by providing threat intelligence, regulatory guidance, and incident response assistance.

The collaboration between governments and the private sector is vital for addressing the complex and evolving nature of cyber threats. By combining regulatory oversight, technological innovation, information sharing, joint training exercises, and critical infrastructure protection efforts, this partnership can create a resilient and proactive cybersecurity ecosystem. As cyber threats continue to grow in sophistication and scale, the synergy between public and private entities will be essential in safeguarding digital assets and maintaining the security of our interconnected world.

www.ingramcontent.com/pod-product-compliance
Lightning Source LLC
Chambersburg PA
CBHW071932210526
45479CB00002B/650